Teen boy's survival guide:

How to build meaningful friendships, confidence, avoid peer pressure and be a man of value.

Robert J. Pond

Table of contents

Chapter 1

Learning good hygiene

As young boys are growing up and learning numerous new things, one of the most essential things that a parent can teach them is self-hygiene. Mostly or generally, it is seen that females tend to maintain their cleanliness to a certain amount. But things are completely contrary when we analyze the situation of lads who, actually do not care much. Especially males who are in middle or high school do not care much about their cleanliness since they are too busy or distracted with so many other things at the time. Thus, at this period parents must provide them some hygiene suggestions for adolescent males and make sure that they practice the same.

Hygiene fundamentally implies how we maintain our bodies clean on a day-to-day basis. This operates in two ways. Firstly, it allows us to be free from germs, if not all at least most of them, and secondly, it aids us in strengthening our social contact with other people. Having high hygiene suggests that you are someone who takes care of themselves.

1.Daily Shower
This may seem a bit unpleasant, but it is the fact of many houses that guys are the ones who required to be reminded on a regular basis about bathing. Boys frequently have the tendency of not caring much and occasionally they may spend weeks without it by relying mostly on somebody's smells or deodorants. Though this is good for a day or two, over a protracted time this may be detrimental for the health as the collected perspiration and dust can lead to various sorts of illness in a different region of the body. Thus, make sure that your adolescent is someone who takes shower on a regular basis without missing it excessively. This

would also aid in keeping his mind fresh and active.

2. Face Wash:

One of the biggest worries for nearly all youngsters is having a face full of acne. And in actuality, this is also one of the most frequent teenage challenges. The biggest reason for this is the neglect of skincare during the teenage years. Teen boys especially suffer from this problem as they hardly take care of their looks. It is vital that a teenager is being taught about cleansing their on regular basis with the use of a suitable face wash or cleanser. And making sure that they do so regularly. While using a specific form of face wash or cleanser teens must remember to be really gentle with their skin and they should massage their face very carefully. In addition, one other thing that nobody informs teens is that they should also massage their face while applying moisturizers. This aids your skin in absorbing the cream or lotion.

3. Use Deodorants:

In teenage years boys take part in different forms of activities each of which involves a lot of body activity and could lead to physical exertion. Because of this, a lot of sweat is formed in the body, which thus needs to be cleaned to make sure that it does not lead to any type of illness or anything. This teenager has to take shower regularly. And along with this youngsters also need to learn to use deodorants or antiperspirants to lessen their sweat. But making sure that they do not use a lot of antiperspirants might lead to the blocking of sweat glands.

4. Oral Hygiene:

There is no doubt in the fact that teens are fairly reckless when it comes to maintaining their oral hygiene. It is vital that young boys brush at least twice a day, floss on a regular basis, and make use of mouthwash now and then. This may aid to prevent or limit the growth of unpleasant bacteria that may enable you to avoid several forms of ailments including cavities and gingivitis. If the teenager ever takes part in a personality development course, then self-hygiene is an important component of it.

5. Clothes and Shaving:
Teen males have the propensity of not changing their clothes on a regular basis and they just keep repeating the same t-shirt without washing. This habit needs to be changed. In addition, during the teenage years, hair growth may be detected in numerous regions of the body. Boys have the want of cleaning that and they demand aid for the same. Make sure you teach young boys about effectively shaving or trimming and many other issues related to it.

6. Clip your nails:
Cut your nails if they are going long with a clipper or manicure scissors. You should also keep them clean by washing them after you wash your hands. Keeping shorter nails

might help you maintain optimum nail cleanliness.

7. Change your clothes frequently:
Wearing unclean clothes may cause germs and bacteria to build up on your body. It's especially crucial to change items that are closest to your body, including undershirts or underwear. Doing this often may prevent your garments from smelling terrible and will keep you clean.
Ideally, attempt to maintain at least five nice shirts and three pairs of slacks that you could wear to school throughout the course of the school week.
You should also change your clothes when you sweat a lot.

8. Keep your feet clean:
Wearing soiled socks, or no socks at all, may cause your feet to smell unpleasant. If you are wearing clean socks but still have a horrible foot odor, concentrate on cleaning them when you shower or bathe and rotate

which shoes you wear during the week. Make sure that your feet are totally dry before putting on socks and shoes.

Putting talcum powder on your feet after you shower might make your feet smell better.

9. Pay attention to your skin and how much you sweat:

Your body changes while you go through puberty and that suggests that many things are happening to you. As you go through adolescence most folks sweat more and their skin could develop more oily

If you realize that you're sweating more, try utilizing underarm antiperspirant to lessen your perspiration.

If you feel that your face is greasy, wash it more regularly with a facial soap developed for oily skin.

10. Wash your hands often:

Get into the habit of washing your hands after going to the toilet, playing outside, or handling anything harboring germs. To prevent being unwell or passing germs to the food you're eating, make sure to wash your hands before and after you eat as well. Consider having a bottle of hand sanitizer with you. Note that this does not replace regular hand washing!

Hygiene is one of the most vital and basic components of daily routine as it makes sure that we are healthy and free from numerous types of diseases and disorders. Thus, it is vital to know various hygiene advice for teenage guys and teach them about the same and execution of the same. Always remember that cleanliness never hurts anyone.

Chapter 2

Puberty

Puberty is a time of development that correlates with your teenage years when you will experience considerable physical growth You may also notice changes in the way you relate with others, and how you view yourself

At different periods you may feel frustrated, excited, and mortified by your changing body — this is all-natural

Parents desiring to assist their kids should endeavor to retain open communication and be hopeful - this is a new and challenging experience for everyone

When does puberty begin?

Puberty is the era when your body matures and goes through remarkable growth. Your body's reproductive system expands, and so too will other internal organs and systems. Your brain also goes through changes during this era that affect your emotions and behaviors.

Puberty begins because of natural substances in your body called hormones. For boys, puberty begins at roughly 11 to 13 years of age and will last for many years. The most key thing to remember is that everyone is different, and you will approach puberty at the correct time for your body, which may be different from other boys in your school.

How will my body change?
When you go through puberty, your body expands as you grow into adulthood. It may even look as though certain changes happen rapidly, but in fact, growth and development generally take place over several years.

There are a few significant alterations to be prepared for.

Growth surge

You will notice that you become taller and that your hands, feet, chest, and shoulders all spread. Some areas may grow faster than others, so if you feel uncomfortable or out of proportion, don't worry, the rest of your body will catch up quickly. Often, boys will go through a growth spurt following their teen years, and you might grow between 10cm and 30cm between the ages of 18 to 20 years. If you discover any growth in your breasts, don't be scared. This is a temporary component of puberty that will most likely go away by itself. If you are anxious, contact your doctor.

Body hair
Hair will begin to grow in your armpits and around your pubic area. It will start to be thin and straight but will get thicker and curlier as you age older. The hair on your arms and legs also gets thicker and darker, and new hair forms on your chin and upper lip. At some moment, you may elect to shave the hair on your face. Every person is

different, and some will acquire more hair than others; look around and observe how all guys seem different from one another, so don't be terrified if you do too.

Genitals
During puberty, your testicles (often known as testes or 'balls') will generate more of a hormone called testosterone. The boost in testosterone encourages further changes in your body, including an increase in the size of your testicles and penis. It's usual for one testicle to grow faster or hang lower than the other — this is nothing to worry about.

Sperm production
Once your testes progress through puberty they will begin to generate more testosterone, which stimulates sperm production. You will start feeling erections and ejaculating when your body releases the sperm from your penis. While this generally happens when you are sexually excited, you may realize that during puberty it seems to

happen for no reason at all. This is common, and generally, people don't notice. You may also wake up to learn that you have undergone an ejaculation while you were sleeping. This is known as a 'wet dream' and is also normal.

Voice

During puberty, your vocal cords develop and your larynx (often known as your Adam's apple) becomes bigger. This causes your voice to 'break' and sound squeaky. Once this has been done, your voice will sound deeper - more like a man's voice.

Other bodily systems

Your brain, bones, organs, and other physiological systems also increase throughout puberty. Your brain will continue to evolve, bringing changes to your behavior. You may witness a shift in your problem-solving and decision-making abilities — for example, your ability to control your urges and make wise decisions.

Your bodily organs, including your limbs, will get larger and stronger, your lung capacity will expand, and your bones and muscles will develop stronger and thicker.

You will also go through various emotional shifts. Learn more about the emotional changes that occur throughout puberty.

Eating healthy and being active is always vital, especially as you take on greater independence and create new habits in this time of your life. Learn more about building healthy habits.

What physical hurdles will I experience throughout puberty?
Voice-breaking
It takes time for your larynx to mature, and you will have a squeaky voice for some time. However, after your vocal cords and larynx have done developing, you will have a

deeper voice and you will sound more like your older male friends and relatives.

Timing

It's common for puberty to begin anytime between the ages of 9 and 14 years old. Everyone is different and there is no way to determine precisely when you will start to see the indicators of puberty. Hormonal changes begin before physical changes and they can't be seen from the outside, so it's easy to conclude that puberty hasn't begun for you since you haven't yet seen the physical changes.

Strength

As your muscles develop and strengthen as you become taller, you may notice that you are more physical than you were before puberty. You might be stronger than you realize, so be mindful not to underestimate your strength.

Skin changes

You may acquire pimples or acne, a skin illness that is frequent throughout and after puberty owing to the hormonal changes occurring at this time. People with acne have spots or lumps on the skin of the face, neck, shoulders, upper back, or chest. There are hundreds of different techniques to manage acne. Maintaining personal cleanliness is always crucial, especially during puberty as your body is developing.

How do my relations with others change?
Emotional changes go hand-in-hand with physical changes. These emotional adjustments allow you to prepare for adult life, relationships, sex, and marriage. You may feel that you crave greater independence from your parents and wish to spend time with friends. You may create a romantic connection with someone or choose to spend more time with companions of a different gender.

It is pretty usual to suddenly feel intense emotions or develop crushes for certain folks. You may decide whether to keep your emotions to yourself, discuss them with a friend or family member, or notify the person directly. Sometimes your sentiments towards someone else — or their feelings towards you — won't be expressed, and this might leave you or them feeling unhappy or rejected. You may choose to discuss this with an older person that you trust about how you feel.

You may also not feel these thoughts, or you may opt to spend time with friends and family, and this is great too.

It may be tough to raise someone who is going through puberty and you may realize that your earlier parenting practices are no longer effective. Maintaining good touch with your youngster and making them feel supported is crucial.

While you should embrace and encourage your kid to take steps towards greater independence, it's OK to have boundaries and expectations. Increased independence comes with increasing responsibility, and establishing clear limits or placing constraints on new activities or habits may help keep kids safe. Not include specific persons in social events.

Taking risky risks while driving.

Using drugs or alcohol.

Shoplifting or theft.

Engaging in sexual activity.

Engaging in bullying or cyberbullying.

Projecting a misleading/false image on social media.

What tactics may assist tackle negative peer pressure?

Pay attention to how you feel. If something doesn't feel right about a scenario, it usually isn't. Even if your pals appear comfortable with what is going on, the scenario may not be appropriate for you.

Plan ahead. Think about how you will react in various scenarios. Plan what you can say or what you can do.

Talk to the individual who is pushing, let him or her know how it makes you feel, and demand the person stop.

Have a secret code to communicate with parents. Something you can say or send to your parent(s) that lets them know you need out of a scenario. Parents may either phone or text to indicate that you need to come home, or that they need to pick you up.

Give an excuse. It should be alright to say "no" without having to apologize or offer an explanation. But it may make it simpler to say no if you have a ready excuse. Perhaps mentioning you have a medical reason such as asthma or allergies that makes it risky for you to ingest anything. Or even suggesting that your parents need you to return home if you believe it would be better to quit the situation all completely.

Have buddies with comparable ideals and ideas. It is simpler to say "no" if someone else is also saying it. Saying "no" jointly makes it simpler for the two of you.

Get help from a trustworthy adult such as a parent, teacher, or school counselor. A trustworthy adult can listen to you and advise you with methods that could work in your circumstance.

Chapter 3

Building self esteem and a good body image

How can I build self-confidence as a teenager?

1. Challenge yourself or throw yourself to such an event where your need to be confident. Even if you lack confidence.

2. Feel delighted when someone underestimates you for your work and says - thank you.

3. Try to stay joyful and have a positive perspective on life.

4. Read optimistic books or like/follow positive pages/persons on social networks.

5. Do prepare for everything which will assist you to stay sure that you have worked on it before presenting/discussing

6. Do remember criticisms are for those who do well. Learn to visualize the difference between criticism and advice

7. Every morning do recollect that you are going to a planet that is in space. Nothing is permanent therefore don't be concerned about what is bad happening around you. Either demotivating deeds or Comparisons.

Where Does Self-Esteem Come From?
Parents, teachers, and others. The individuals in our lives may affect how we feel about ourselves. When they focus on what's excellent about us, we feel good about ourselves. When people are patient when we make blunders, we learn to accept ourselves. When we have friends and get along, we feel like.

But if adults rebuke more than they praise, it's impossible to feel good about oneself. Bullying and brutal mocking by siblings or peers may impair self-esteem, too. Harsh statements may stick, and become part of how you think about yourself. Luckily, it doesn't have to stay that way.

The voice in your head. The things you speak to yourself have a tremendous influence on how you feel about yourself. Thinking, "I'm such a loser" or "I'll never make friends," lowers your self-esteem.

There are numerous ways to think about the same subjects. "I didn't win this time — but maybe next time." "Maybe I can make some mates." That voice is more upbeat. It helps you feel OK. And it could turn out to be true.

Sometimes, the voice in our minds is based on terrible words others have uttered. Or on horrific things, we have encountered. Sometimes, the voice is merely us being hard on ourselves. But we can adjust the voice in our brains. We can learn to think better of ourselves.

Learning to do things. We feel happy when we learn to read, add, draw, or create. Perform a sport, play music, write an essay, ride a bike. Set the table, and wash the car. Help a pal, walk the dog. Each thing you learn and do is a chance to feel good about yourself. Step back and analyze what you can accomplish. Let yourself feel satisfied with it.

But sometimes we're too severe on ourselves. We don't accept that what we do is good enough. If we believe, "It's not any good," "It's not perfect," or "I can't do it well enough," we lose the opportunity to generate self-esteem.

What If My Self-Esteem Is Low?
You may do things to feel better about yourself. It's never too late. Here are some techniques to boost your self-esteem:

Be with those who treat you properly. Some people act in ways that knock you down. Others pull you up by what they say and do. Learn to tell the difference. Choose folks who help you feel OK about yourself. Find folks you can be yourself with. Be that sort of friend for others.

Say helpful things to yourself. Tune in to the voice in your head. Is it unduly critical? Are you too harsh on yourself? For a few days, jot down some of the things you say to yourself. Look over your list. Are these things you'd say to a close friend? If not, rewrite them in a way that's honest, fair, and kind. Read your new phrases periodically. Do that until it's more of a habit to think that way.

Accept what's not perfect. It's always wonderful to do the best you can. But when you think you need to be faultless, you can't feel good about anything less. Accept your best. Let yourself feel comfortable about it.

Ask for assistance if you can't move beyond a desire to be flawless.

Set objectives and strive toward them. If you want to feel good about yourself, pursue things that are useful for you. Maybe you wish to eat a healthier diet, get more active, or study better. Make a goal. Then develop a plan on how to accomplish it. Stick with your plan. Track your progress. Be proud of what you've done so far. Say to yourself, "I've been following my plan to work out every day for 45 minutes. I feel alright with it. I know I can keep it up."

Focus on what goes well. Are you so used to talking about challenges that they're all you see? It's easy to get caught up in what's wrong. But unless you balance it with what's good, it merely makes you feel bad. Next time, catch yourself when you grumble about yourself or your day. Find something that went well instead.

Give and aid. Giving is one of the greatest techniques to boost self-esteem. Tutor a student, help clean up your town or walk for a good cause. Help out at home or school. Make it a habit to be polite and fair. Do things that make you proud of the type of person you are. When you undertake things that make a difference (even a modest one) your self-esteem will increase.

Do you ever wish you could modify anything about your body? If so, you're not alone. Lots of people feel unhappy with some components of their characteristics. But when you become hooked on things you don't like, it may severely suck down your self-esteem.

You don't need a faultless physique to have a great body image. When you appreciate your body as it is, right now, you boost your body image. And your self-esteem too.

But what if I need to be in better shape? Some folks feel, "When I get in better shape, I'll love my body. But it's smarter to start the other way. First, accept your body. Find something to like about it. Take fantastic care of your body. When you appreciate your body, it's easy to care for it right.

Want to look and feel your best? Here are some tips:

Accept Your Body
Nobody's perfect. Everybody wants to be liked and accepted just as they are. That's true for every BODY, too! See your body the way it is. Be less of a critic. Be more of a friend.

Don't body-shame yourself. When you make harsh judgments about your own body, it lowers your self-esteem. That's true whether you say it out loud or think it to yourself. It hurts just as much as if someone else said it.

Be polite. Respect yourself, even if you have issues to work on.

Build a healthy habit. Do you have a propensity of putting your body down? To break that bad habit, develop a positive one as its substitute. Tell yourself what you appreciate instead of what you don't. Keep doing it until it is a habit.

Like Your Body
Find something to appreciate about your looks. Maybe you like your hair, face, or hands. What about your form, shoulders, or legs? Your eyes or your smile? Tell yourself what you appreciate and why. If you are trapped, think about what your fantastic buddies appreciate about how you seem. Accept those things. Know that there are lots to love about you. Let yourself feel great.

Focus on what your body can DO. There's more to your body than your looks. When you play a sport, walk, run, dance, swim - that's your body in action. Your body is there for you when you stretch, reach, climb, or jump for joy. When you carry things, manufacture things, or hug someone. Be impressed. Be appreciative.

Be attentive to your body. Don't overlook your body as you travel through the day. Learn to breathe lightly and quietly as you exercise and stretch. Learn to identify when your body needs food or rest. Enjoy the way your body feels when you walk, run, and play.

Take Care of Your Body
Eat wholesome meals. Learn what foods are healthy for you, and how much is the correct number. Take your time as you eat. Taste your food. Enjoy it. Eating healthily helps you look your best. It provides you with the vitality you need. And it boosts your body image. When you treat your body properly, you feel good about yourself.

Get good sleep. Learn how much sleep you need for your age. Get to bed on time. Turn off screens hours before night so you can sleep well.

Be active every day. Your body needs to move to be strong, fit, and healthy. You may be active by playing a sport. You may run, walk, work out, conduct yoga, swim, or dance. Pick activities you like. Enjoy the fun you can have.

Keep at a healthy weight. Being a healthy weight is vital for you. And it helps you feel good about your body. But don't try to diet on your own. Always talk to your parent or doctor. Your doctor can offer techniques so you can remain at a weight that's healthy for you.

What If I Need Help With My Body Image and Self-Esteem?

Sometimes, body image or self-esteem concerns are too much to confront alone. Health challenges, unhappiness, or trauma may influence how you feel about yourself. Eating disorders may develop a poor body image that isn't real.

Tell a parent, doctor, or therapist what you're going through. Ask for help. Body image and self-esteem may become enhanced with instruction and care.

Chapter 4

Preparation for college

What does it mean to be ready for college? There are certain key actions to take throughout high school. Here are recommendations to enable you to be prepared intellectually and personally for your college experience.

Start Planning for College Now!

Take the Right High School Classes to Prepare for College

Get Involved in Extracurricular Activities

Keep an Extracurricular Record

Get to Know your High School Guidance Counselor

Build Relationships with Mentors

Work on College Readiness Life Skills

College Visits – Schedule a College Campus Tour

College Entrance Exams - Make a Plan

Create an Organization System

Apply for College Admission, Financial Aid, and Scholarships

High School is a terrific time to study, explore, grow, and dream. When you start your freshman year, you may not know where you want to go to college or what you want to study. But there are things you can do that will advance you towards being ready to pick, apply, and get admitted to a wonderful institution. You need to be prepared for the hurdles you will experience once you arrive and start your college career. The following advice and information will help you prepare for academic success in college.

1. Start Planning for College Now!

If you are a high school student, or will soon be a high school student, now is the time to start planning for your post-secondary education. College may feel like it's far away, but in some respects, it will be here before you know it! Preparing for a college degree involves time, work, and attention.

When should I start preparing for college?

High school presents numerous chances, but it is up to you to make use of them. You may make the most of your high school years by looking forward and learning how to prepare for the future. Take the initial step and make up your mind that you will make the most of the next years, knowing your efforts will pay off later!

2. Take the Right High School Classes to Prepare for College

Plan to work hard in high school. Taking the most rigorous courses available can help you in various ways. In addition to learning the course material, such as Algebra, Chemistry, or a foreign language, college preparation programs will help enhance your abilities in note-taking, studying, writing, test-taking, time management, critical thinking, and more. These vital abilities will prepare you for the difficulty of a college education.

How can I prepare for college academically?
Many high schools offer Advanced Placement (AP) programs, and some offer International Baccalaureate (IB) courses or Dual Enrollment possibilities, which have the extra advantage of enabling you to obtain college credit. Dual credit for IB and AP courses is dependent on taking the equivalent IB Higher Level examination or AP exam after the course. The needed score to receive dual credit can vary from institution to college. Depending on your score and your desired major, the given

college credit may enable you to forgo a class, start in the next course level, or complete optional courses.

Some high schools may provide "weight" to your Grade Point Average (GPA) for advanced programs such as AP or Honors, thus taking these classes can raise your GPA. Another benefit of taking AP, IB, Dual Enrollment, or Honors level classes is that the class is marked as such on your high school transcript and schools will know that you choose to push yourself intellectually. This motivation indicates a college board that you are more prepared for the college classroom.

One word of caution: These sorts of courses are demanding. Know yourself! Don't take a class if you are not prepared to perform pretty well with hard work and effort. It is extremely crucial to take Dual Enrollment programs seriously since these college credits and strong grades will be a part of your college transcript.

There are so many options for courses. How do I select between them?
Develop your intellectual interest. Especially during your junior and senior years of high school, you may typically take classes that will prepare you for the college degree program of your choosing. For example, if you are contemplating nursing school, it might be advantageous (or perhaps needed for entrance) to study subjects such as Anatomy, Physiology, or Statistics in high school.

Thinking about an engineering degree? Load up on math and science courses. You don't have to know precisely what major you will select but completing courses in your primary area of academic interest will best equip you to expand upon that knowledge in college.

3. Get Involved in Extracurricular Activities

Involvement in activities outside of coursework makes high school a lot more fascinating and entertaining. These extracurricular activities also allow obtaining proficiencies you couldn't learn from textbooks and assessments alone. Through extracurricular activities, you may acquire key abilities, such as collaboration, public speaking, creativity, leadership, and self-awareness.

What extracurricular activities should I undertake in high school?

The first step is to investigate. As you attend high school, you will discover you have many new opportunities—sports, theater, music, art, debate, and computer science, just to mention a few. While you can't do everything, try to become involved in as many groups, teams, and events as you find fascinating. There is not a mandatory one-size-fits-all list of activities—what counts is that you select groups and programs that interest you!

You won't know whether you like something if you don't try it. Keep a look out for groups that may especially assist you to prepare for a certain college major. For example, if you think you may be interested in pursuing a business degree, While you want to look "well rounded," it is crucial that you don't take on too much. Allow yourself enough time to flourish at the things you care about most. It might be good to regard freshman year as the time to try a variety of things. In your sophomore year, you might begin restricting your commitment to your most significant activities. This will enable you to spend more time on fewer things.

Ask yourself these critical questions: What is most important to you? How do you grow that area into a real passion? How can you take your engagement to the next level? How do you become an expert, a leader, or raise community awareness in that area? This is what makes you special and helps you to shine on a college application or qualify for a scholarship. Developing an interest into a passion may also drive you towards an area of study and choice of job.

4. Keep an Extracurricular Record
Keep a record of your extracurricular activities. You might be asked about them in a few different ways on college applications. Your high school will keep track of your coursework, grades, and credits. It is up to you to keep track of everything else.

In order to be prepared for college applications, establish a document that documents your activity in sports, groups, volunteer work, community service, part-time jobs, etc., and maintain it in one place. Begin with the summer following eighth grade (you were a high school student at that time) and continue through your senior year. Keep note of the time you spend on each activity and look for patterns that reflect your engagement in worthwhile activities. Don't forget to capture any accolades, honors, and leadership positions. This list will be tremendously helpful—not just while you are applying to universities, but also for scholarship applications or developing a résumé. If you wait until your senior year, it is incredibly tough to recall everything you did. As the Chinese adage suggests, "Your memory is only as good as the paper you write it on."

5. Get to Know your High School Guidance Counselor

You presumably have a high school guidance counselor assigned to you. Make an appointment with him or her! You don't need to wait till people reach out to you. It is crucial to contact your guidance counselor often, beginning with your freshman year.

Who can help me get prepared for college?

Your guidance counselor understands your school options and possibilities, including visits from college admissions counselors, college fairs, test prep programs, scholarships, and much more. Your guidance counselor is also a terrific resource for social and emotional assistance as well as career and college preparedness.

Unfortunately, most guidance counselors are incredibly busy and overworked. Make their task as simple as possible. Come to your session with your questions ready and don't anticipate spending too much time at each visit. Thank your guidance counselor for the information, aid, and advice. Remember that you may require a letter of reference from your guidance counselor. To produce an effective letter, your guidance counselor has to know your finest attributes and also what shines out about you.

It might be beneficial to think about your guidance counselor as you would think of your doctor. They are busy, they care about you, they know a lot, and they offer you advice. It is crucial to heed their advice—though when in doubt, it's always smart to acquire a second opinion.

6. Build Relationships with Mentors
Coaches, teachers, employers, and religious leaders are all potential mentors who can provide valuable support. Look for individuals who make you exclaim, "I want to be like them when I grow up!" or "I want to do that career when I graduate." Get to know them and discover more about their life. Learn from their errors and their accomplishments. Share your ambitions and worries with them and seek guidance about picking a college and profession.

Mentors can open up prospects for you, and may help you discover your talents (and faults!). A mentor will offer methods to grow and give insight while making choices. You might also ask your mentor to write a letter of reference. Building connections with mentors is a talent you will acquire throughout your life. Start now. And ideally, you can be a mentor for someone else someday!

7. Work on College Readiness Life Skills
How can I become ready for college life?
Make a list of the life skills you would want to acquire, then keep adding to it. Think over the ideal approach for you to learn about each talent. Can your dad teach you to prepare your favorite meal? Can your neighbor teach you how to check your oil or replace a tire? Can your mum teach you the fundamentals of washing laundry? Can your instructor or mentor help you develop short-term objectives and build a strategy to attain them? What about food shopping, money management, and personal safety? Some things you can teach yourself, like remembering to set your alarm clock so you get up on time. Many talents you may acquire simply by viewing a lesson online.

Depending on the number of life skills you wish to master, establish a strategy and set a goal— such as learning and practicing one new ability per month.

8. College Visits - Schedule a College Campus Tour

Try to visit as many college campuses as possible early on during your high school years. Don't wait to do every visit during your senior year. While it is ideal to visit during the academic year when campus life is busy, a visit in the summer is better than no visit at all, and a campus visit can be readily added to most summer vacation travels. Campus visits might vary from a few hours to an entire day, but normally expect to spend an afternoon.

9. College Entrance Exams - Make a Plan

Make no mistake, colleges, and institutions regard college admission examinations to be one of the most essential new student standards. Familiarize yourself with regular college admission examinations and what is necessary or suggested by the universities that interest you. U.S. institutions will typically accept the ACT or the SAT, however, some may favor one over the other. Some institutions additionally encourage or require the optional essay section of the tests. You will need to determine which exam you will take, and some students take both standardized tests. It is ideal to take college admission examinations during your junior year, however, some determined high school sophomores may take the tests merely to see how they perform and as part of their preparation.

How can I prepare to take the SAT or ACT test?
There are no quick shortcuts. The best approach to prepare for college admission examinations like the SAT or ACT is to take a hard curriculum while in high school and to understand the content thoroughly. For

example, the greatest approach to prepare for the math component of the ACT or SAT is to study math! Beyond that, it is useful to practice and discover strategies to help you achieve your best. Ask your guidance counselor for tips that are particular to you and how you test. He or she may be able to propose particular test prep sessions or tutors beneficial for the SAT and ACT tests.

Many students need to acquire tactics for pacing themselves as the examinations are timed. If the initial test doesn't go as well as you hoped, don't give up. Many students choose to take the entrance exams more than once. You may utilize your earlier results to concentrate on your preparation for the upcoming exam. For example, if math was your lowest score, spend time studying for that component of the examination.

Set a goal to finish your final SAT or ACT exam by the summer following your junior year. That will enable you to send your exam results to the schools at the beginning of your senior year.

10. Create an Organization System

How to keep organized researching colleges?

As soon as you start meeting with college representatives and touring universities, you will receive crucial information you'll need to remain organized. If you can't visit a campus in person, you may learn a lot by "visiting" a college online and examining its website. Information aggregation websites like U.S. News, Niche, Chegg, and others may also be utilized to study various schools and institutions. Create a document where you may record crucial facts, so you don't forget. If you discover a school that offers a certain major, jot it down. If you hear of a Study Abroad program that seems wonderful, add this to your notes. If you had a nice campus tour, be sure to post your experiences. Make a note of anything that excites you and is essential to you so you don't forget. Include comments regarding scholarships, internship programs, instructors, research initiatives, outdoor possibilities, campus groups, and more.

As you progress towards your senior year, you will reduce your choice of institutions that you believe are the greatest match for you. All the facts you have gathered—as well as all the self-discovery you have earned throughout high school—will help you make the greatest choice.

11. Apply for College Admission, Financial Aid, and Scholarships

Once you've developed a list of your top universities, create a new document (or re-organize the document you used to record relevant college information) to aid you throughout the application and admissions process. Make notes of any application dates, rules, and any other needs. If you requested professors and mentors for letters of reference, establish reminders to follow up and check the college has received them.

Plan time into your calendar before the start of your senior year so you may fully focus on your college applications, as well as explore financial assistance and scholarships. Remember that financial help might include not just scholarships and grants (money you don't have to return) but also loans (that you do have to repay) (that you do have to repay). If you'll require part-time employment, you may explore university jobs to uncover various options. This critical study will help you establish a strategy to pay for education.

Are you ready for College?
Make every effort to meet with and learn from your guidance counselors, mentors, and other role models in your life. Allow these trustworthy and prominent role

models to assist you to enhance your talents and discover inventive methods to work on your flaws. Stay organized and take notes while you investigate institutions and apply for admissions. Once you go to college, you will continue to develop, learn and improve in all of your academic objectives. The time you spend on college preparation and the effort you put in now will establish the basis for academic achievement and a lifetime of study.

Printed in Great Britain
by Amazon

15567342R00037